OCS Study MMS 2005-057

Final Report

Importance of the Alaskan Beaufort Sea to King Eiders (*Somateria spectabilis*)

Principal Investigator: Abby N. Powell, Ph.D.
                           Research Associate Professor
                           Institute of Arctic Biology
                           University of Alaska Fairbanks
                               and Research Wildlife Biologist, USGS
                           Alaska Cooperative Fish and Wildlife Research Unit

Co-principal Investigator: Laura Phillips, M. S.
                           Dept. Biology and Wildlife
                           University of Alaska Fairbanks

Co-principal Investigator: Eric A. Rexstad, Ph.D.
                           Associate Professor
                           Institute of Arctic Biology
                           University of Alaska Fairbanks

Co-principal Investigator: Eric J. Taylor, Ph.D.
                           Fish and Wildlife Biologist
                           U.S. Fish and Wildlife Service
                               and Research Associate
                           Institute of Arctic Biology
                           University of Alaska Fairbanks

Prepared by Laura Phillips

August 2005

LIST OF TABLES

LIST OF FIGURES

ABSTRACT

Alaskan-breeding king eiders (*Somateria spectabilis*) molt wing feathers and over winter in remote areas of the Bering Sea, precluding direct observation. This study employed the use of satellite telemetry to determine areas used by king eiders throughout the annual cycle. We collected location data of 60 individuals (27 females and 33 males) over three years (2002–2004) from satellite telemetry. More than 80% of our transmittered eiders spent more than 2 weeks staging offshore prior to beginning molt migration, suggesting that the sea is an important migration flyway and staging area for this species. During post-breeding staging and migration, male king eiders had much broader distributions in the Alaskan Beaufort Sea than female eiders, which were concentrated in Harrison and Smith Bays. Distribution of locations did not vary by sex during spring migration. Significant variation in residence time in the Beaufort Sea was explained by sex with female king eiders spending more days within the sea than males during post-breeding and spring migrations. Shorter residence times of eiders and deeper water depths at locations during spring migration suggest the Alaskan Beaufort Sea may not be as critical a staging area for king eiders in spring as it is post-breeding. Distributions of molt and winter locations did not differ by sex or among years. We recommend managers minimize disturbance of core use areas in Harrison and Smith Bays during post-breeding and future studies examine the importance of potential spring staging areas outside the Alaskan Beaufort Sea.

INTRODUCTION

King eiders (*Somateria spectabilis*) spend the majority of their annual cycle in remote marine habitats, precluding direct observation and contributing to an incomplete understanding of their life histories. King eiders perform wing molt, fall, and spring migrations during the nonbreeding period (Suydam 2000), and presumably this migratory behavior has evolved as an advantage to provide the greatest potential reproductive success for individuals (Baker 1978). This study was developed with two broad objectives: (1) to determine the use of the Beaufort Sea as a flyway and staging area, and (2) to provide an initial description of the migration ecology of king eiders breeding on Alaska's North Slope.

Alaskan-breeding king eiders disperse from nesting areas on the Arctic Coastal Plain and move through the Beaufort Sea to wing molt and wintering locations in the Bering Sea. Hundreds of thousands of king eiders use the Alaskan Beaufort Sea as a flyway, staging, or molting area each year (Thomson and Person 1963, Woodby and Divoky 1982, Suydam et al. 2000). Development of offshore oil and gas resources on natural and artificial islands in the Beaufort Sea has prompted managers to fund baseline studies about the distribution of king eiders in the sea. These data are critical to model potential consequences from oil spills and to provide regulatory agencies with opportunities to modify proposed developments and associated activities to minimize impacts. Potential impacts from oil spills may include displacement of eiders from foraging habitat, contamination of food resources, and mortality from oiling (Flint et al. 1999, Stehn and Platte 2000).

After leaving the Beaufort Sea, king eiders migrate to marine areas where they congregate in flocks and molt all flight feathers. During this three-to-four week flightless period, movements are constrained, and eiders may be vulnerable to disturbance and predation, and subject to higher energy demands (Salomonsen 1968, King 1974, Hohman et al. 1992). Post-molting king eiders then migrate to wintering areas that are generally characterized by short periods of daylight and extremes in weather conditions, temperature, and ice cover (Systad et al. 2000, Petersen and Douglas 2004). Eiders generally form pair bonds on these wintering areas and migrate as pairs to breeding grounds in the spring (Anderson et al. 1992).

The chronology of these life-history events during the nonbreeding period may be linked to productivity on the breeding grounds (Heitmeyer and Fredrickson 1981, Hepp 1984, Dugger 1997), and may vary by age, sex, and habitat condition (Heitemeyer 1988). This may be especially true for eiders due to their heavy reliance on endogenous reserves for egg laying (Korschgen 1977, Kellet 1999). Concern regarding apparent population declines in recent years of all four eider species (Stehn et al. 1993, Suydam et al. 2000) has led to increased interest in location and timing of migration, definition of wing molt and wintering areas, and habitat characterization of these sites (U.S. Fish and Wildlife Service 1999, Sea Duck Joint Venture Management Board 2001).

In this study, we obtained location data for the entire annual cycle of 33 king eiders in 2002 and 2003. Additionally, we collected wing molt location information for 27 eiders in 2004. Thus, we can model the areas of the Alaskan Beaufort Sea used by king eiders during spring migration and post-breeding and describe the movements of king eiders throughout the nonbreeding period.

The original objectives of this study were to: (1) document movements and locations of spring, summer, and fall migrating adult female king eiders (successful and unsuccessful breeders) marked on breeding areas on the North Slope of Alaska; (2) describe potential staging areas used during spring and fall migration; (3) determine if adult female king eiders molt in the Beaufort Sea prior to migration to overwintering areas; (4) describe sea ice and open water conditions of the Beaufort Sea relative to observed locations of satellite implanted king eiders.

Due to logistical limitations on our ability to trap king eiders on breeding grounds in summer and the inherent low annual reproductive success of this species, we did not obtain a sample of female king eiders that successfully raised young to fledgings. We were also not able to obtain information on the nesting status of the females using transmitters prior to egg laying. Due to these limitations, we restrict our analyses to only unsuccessful female and male king eiders.

Satellite imagery of sea ice in the Beaufort Sea was not available at intervals frequent enough for useful description of conditions in the Beaufort Sea relative to king eider locations. However, we describe water depth and distance offshore of king eider locations within the Beaufort Sea and determine explanatory variables that describe variation in the number of days king eiders spend within the sea.

To address the above objectives, we will examine the distribution and use areas of king eiders while in the Beaufort Sea, during spring and fall staging, and during wing molt and winter; describe the timing of migratory movements; and describe characteristics of king eider locations within the Beaufort Sea.

METHODS

Trapping Sites

We trapped king eiders in early to mid-June of 2002, 2003, and 2004 at two sites on the North Slope of Alaska, Teshekpuk Lake (70°26'N, 153°08'W) and Kuparuk (70°20'N, 149°45'W). The Kuparuk study site was located between the Colville and Kuparuk Rivers. The Teshekpuk Lake study site was added as a trapping location in 2004 and was located about 80 km west of the Kuparuk study area and 10 km inland from the southeast shore of Teshekpuk Lake.

Beaufort Sea

During the post-breeding period (late June through mid-September), Alaskan-breeding king eiders move into the Beaufort Sea where they stage or begin migration to wing molt locations. The Beaufort Sea is part of the Arctic Ocean that lies north of Alaska from Point Barrow eastward to Banks Island north of the Yukon and Northwest Territories of Canada. It has a narrow continental shelf that extends an average of 55 km offshore to the 200 m bathymetric contours (Soluri and Woodson 1990). Sea ice generally covers the entire sea for 9 to 10 months each year. Nearshore ice freezes to the seafloor in winter and ice scouring of benthic habitats nearshore can be severe (Barnes et al. 1984). Primary productivity is low, and food webs are relatively simple with secondary biological productivity peaking during the ice-free summer months of June through October (Norton and Weller 1984).

Bering Sea

During wing molt migration (late June through mid-September), Alaskan-breeding king eiders generally move into the Bering Sea. The Bering Sea is characterized by a large, shallow, gently-sloping coastal shelf that is less than 200 m deep and encompasses almost half the sea's total area. This shelf is broad in the east (>500 km) along the Alaskan coast and narrow (<100 km) in the west along the Siberian coast.

In winter, the Bering Sea is characterized by high winds, frequent storms, and complete ice coverage of its shallow continental shelf region (Niebauer et al. 1999). The seasonal ice pack persists for six to eight months each year and generally reaches its maximum southern extent by March or April (Fay 1974). Major polynyas occur downwind of the Chukchi Peninsula, St. Lawrence Island, St. Matthew Island, and the Seward Peninsula (Stringer and Groves 1991). The amount of available daylight in the Bering Sea decreases to between four and six hours in late December and early January.

The Bering Sea is unusually productive for a high latitude body of water. A number of mechanisms are thought to support this high productivity, including the broad shallow coastal shelf, the extensive seasonal ice coverage, and the convergence of current systems rich in nutrients (Springer and McRoy 1993). The high density of benthic invertebrates in the Bering Sea is thought to be linked to its high primary productivity (Grebmeier 1993). King eiders probably forage on benthic and epibenthic invertebrates while in marine systems (Frimer 1997, Suydam 2000).

Capture and Telemetry

We obtained locations of king eiders throughout the nonbreeding period using implantable satellite transmitters. We captured king eiders on breeding grounds in early to mid-June using mist net arrays and decoys. Once captured, eiders were placed in a secure, dark kennel and transported to an indoor facility or weatherport equipped for surgery. A 35-g satellite platform transmitting terminal (PTT) transmitter (Microwave Telemetry, Inc., Columbia, Maryland) was surgically implanted into the abdominal cavity of each eider following the techniques of Korschgen et al. (1996). Satellite transmitters were <3% of the average body mass of birds used in this study. Surgeries generally took 20 minutes to complete. We held birds until fully awake and recovered from anesthesia (2 – 3 h), and then released them at their capture sites. If both the male and female of a pair were captured simultaneously, we released the pair together at the capture site. At Kuparuk, transmitters were implanted into 21 (10 female, 11 male) king eiders in 2002, 12 (3 female, 9 male) in 2003, and 15 (8 female, 7 male) in 2004. We fitted 12 (5 female, 7 male) king eiders with transmitters at Teshekpuk in 2004. Eiders were fitted with a U.S. Fish and Wildlife Service band while still under anesthesia. All methods and handling of birds were approved by the University of Alaska Institutional Animal Care and Use Committee (IACUC # 02-10). There were no fatalities within three months of surgery.

To maximize location and duration of wing molt and location duration and timing of molt migration, transmitters were programmed with four duty cycles. Transmitters were on and transmitting location information to satellites for six hours every 48 h from June through September, every 84 h from October through December, every 168 h from January through March, and every 84 h from April until the end of the battery life. The expected battery life was about one year. Satellite transmitters used in this study had an average life-span of 385 ± 15 (SE) days ($n = 33$, range 99 – 519 days). We received location data from Service Argos (2001). Error associated with satellite telemetry locations has been estimated by Service Argos (2001) to be $\leq$ 1km for locations with a location class of at least 0 and < 150 m for locations with a class of 3; however, a study by Britten et al. (1999) estimated an average error of 4 km for 0 class locations from small (30g) backpack-mounted satellite transmitters. There is no published information on the accuracy of the 35g implantable satellite transmitters used in this study. Location data was filtered for accuracy using PC-SAS Argos Filter V6.4 (Dave Douglas, USGS, Alaska Science Center, Anchorage, AK). The filtering program removed implausible locations based on location redundancy and tracking paths. For our analyses, the best location per transmission period was used based on location class to ensure independence of locations. Locations were plotted using ArcView GIS (ESRI 1998). Definitions used to categorize events throughout the annual cycle for use in analyses are included in Table 1.

Table 1. Definitions of King Eider nonbreeding life history events as defined by satellite telemetry locations.

Definition	
Migration	*A set of sequential locations indicating movement in a single direction during which an individual remains in one area > 1 week (Petersen et al. 1999)*
Wing molt migration	*The migration period from the last day at the breeding area to the first day at the wing molt location*
Wing molt site	*An area where an eider spent ≥ 3 weeks with lowest daily movement rates between June and December prior to movement toward wintering areas*
Fall migration	*The migration period from the last day at the wing molt site to the first day at the farthest south wintering location*
Wintering area	*An area where an eider spent > 1 week between the end of the wing molt period and spring migration; King Eiders may have multiple wintering areas*
Spring migration	*The period of migration from the last day at a wintering area to the first day on land at a subsequent breeding location; if there were no onshore locations for an eider during the subsequent breeding period, the first location at a June offshore staging area was used*
Subsequent breeding area	*An area onshore where an individual was located after spring migration and prior to fall migration*

Data Analysis

Distribution and Use Areas

Beaufort Sea. We used fixed kernel analysis (Seaman et al. 1998) to delineate king eider use areas in the Beaufort Sea. We considered the 95% utilization distribution to represent an estimate of total distribution, and the contour representing greater than average observed density as the core use area. Due to the variation in the number of locations obtained per individual in the Alaskan Beaufort Sea (range: 1 – 44 locations), we randomly selected a subset of locations based on the average number of locations received per individual within a season to ensure kernel distributions reflected the distribution of our sample of individuals rather than any one individual eider. We randomly selected 10 post-breeding locations (June – September) and 7 spring locations (April – July) per individual to create 2 subsets of eider locations for use in kernel analyses.

10

Differences in distributions of king eider locations in the Beaufort Sea were examined using multiresponse permutation procedures (MRPP) in BLOSSOM (USGS, Fort Collins, Colorado; Cade and Richards 2001). We examined differences by sex and season (spring vs. post-breeding), and among years. We also compared 2004 post-breeding distributions of male and female king eiders transmittered at Kuparuk to those captured at Teshekpuk. Because MRPP is sensitive to large differences in sample sizes, we randomly selected a subset of locations from larger samples when necessary to make sample sizes equivalent.

Post-breeding and spring staging. Staging areas of king eiders during wing molt and spring migrations were described. Spring staging areas were defined as areas where eiders spent ≥ 1 week during spring migration, and post-breeding staging areas were defined as areas where king eiders spent ≥ 1 week during wing molt migration.

Wing molt and winter. Latitudes of wing molt and wintering sites were calculated as the centroid of minimum convex polygons (Hooge and Eichenlaub 1997) at these sites. Differences in distributions of king eiders during the wing molt and winter periods were examined using multiresponse permutation procedures (MRPP) in BLOSSOM (USGS, Fort Collins, Colorado, Cade and Richards 2001). We used the centroid of the minimum convex polygon (Hooge and Eichenlaub 1997) of the wing molt area and farthest south wintering area of each individual as the sampling unit and compared distributions by sex and among years.

Movements

We used two-way ANOVA to test for differences by sex and year in the timing of molt migration, residence at wing molt sites, fall migration, and spring migration. Significant differences among years were further examined using Tukey multiple comparison procedures. We calculated migration distance as the distance between as many subsequent locations that passed filtering requirements as possible per individual and corrected for curvature of the earth. Latitude of wing molt and wintering sites was calculated as the centroid of minimum convex polygons (Hooge and Eichenlaub 1997) created in ArcView GIS using Lambert Equal Area Azimuthal projection.

Beaufort Sea Location Characteristics

We used two-way ANOVA on ranked data to test for differences by sex and season in water depth and distance from shore of eider locations. Water depth at eider locations was calculated using a bathymetric shapefile with 10-m contour intervals compiled by the Alaska Science Center (1997). Distance from shore was calculated using ArcView GIS as the distance from an eider location to a 1:250,000 polyline shapefile (Soluri and Woodson 1990) of the Alaskan coastline. Because distance from shore and water depth were significantly correlated ($r_s = 0.614$, $P < 0.001$), we report results from water depth analysis only.

Variation in the number of days an eider spent in the Alaskan Beaufort Sea was examined using multiple regression. Residence time of a king eider was calculated as the number of days from the first day an eider entered the sea until the date of the last location within the sea. Explanatory variables within the model included sex, season (post-breeding vs. spring), year, and standardized Julian date of an individual's first location within Beaufort Sea. Julian date of an eider's first location within the sea was standardized to allow season to be included in the analysis as a class variable. Standardized Julian date was calculated as the difference between the Julian day of an individual's first location within the Beaufort Sea and the Julian day the first transmittered eider arrived in the sea each season. We included the first order interaction terms sex with season, year, and standardized Julian date.

RESULTS

Distribution and Use Areas

Beaufort Sea. Distributions of king eider locations during spring did not differ among years (δ_{149} = -0.70, P = 0.16). Distributions of male locations during post-breeding did not differ among years (δ_{258} = -1.54, P = 0.079). Post-breeding distribution of female locations in 2003 differed significantly from those in 2002 (δ_{58} = -6.41, P < 0.001) and 2004 (δ_{58} = -5.79, P = 0.001); however, 2002 and 2004 distributions did not differ (δ_{60} = 0.81, P = 0.99).

Distributions of king eider locations in the Alaskan Beaufort Sea differed by sex during the post-breeding period (δ_{516} = -26.38, P < 0.001), but not during spring migration (δ_{41} = -1.67, P = 0.068). Female locations tended to be concentrated in Harrison Bay and Smith Bay during post-breeding, while male locations were more widely dispersed in the Alaskan Beaufort Sea from Oliktok Point to Point Barrow (Figure 1).

Spring and post-breeding distributions of eiders differed significantly (δ_{91} = -26.36, P < 0.001). Spring locations were scattered from Point Barrow to the Canadian border with over 40% of the locations found > 20 km offshore. Core use areas during the post-breeding period were located nearshore and distributed uniformly between the Kuparuk capture site and Point Barrow (Figure 2).

The post-breeding distributions of male and female king eiders captured at Kuparuk differed significantly from distributions of those captured at Teshekpuk (male δ_{94} = -10.64, P < 0.001, female δ_{86} = -17.70, P < 0.001). Females from Kuparuk were concentrated in Harrison Bay while core use areas of Teshekpuk females were located in Smith Bay. Locations of male eiders captured at Teshekpuk Lake were widely dispersed in the Beaufort Sea which resulted in a large core use area that covered the majority of the continental shelf from Point Barrow to Harrison Bay. Males captured at Kuparuk were more concentrated in small areas resulting in scattered dense core use areas off Oliktok Point and in Harrison and Smith Bays (Figure 3).

Post-breeding and spring staging. Post-breeding staging areas for male and female king eiders included the Alaskan Beaufort Sea, Ledyard Bay, and the Chukotsk Peninsula (Figure 4).

Spring staging areas for king eiders in this study were located outside the Alaskan Beaufort Sea in the Chukchi Sea and Canadian Beaufort Sea. All transmittered eiders returning to the arctic coastal plain of Alaska and Canada in spring staged in Ledyard Bay in the Chukchi Sea prior to entering the Beaufort Sea. Female king eiders exhibited fidelity to nesting areas by returning to sites near the capture site. Male king eiders migrated to Russia, Alaska, and Canada in the spring, presumably following females to their breeding grounds. Five of 15 males returning to breeding areas in the spring appeared to forego breeding and staged offshore in the Canadian Beaufort Sea (Figure 4).

Wing molt and winter. During wing molt, king eiders were located in areas along the Chukotsk, Kamchatka, and Alaska Peninsulas, as well as St. Lawrence Island, Anadyr, Olyutor, Karagin, Bristol and Kuskokwim Bays, the Beaufort Sea, and the coast of Russia near Khatyrka (Table 2, Figure 5). In 2002, one female molted wing feathers in the Alaskan Beaufort Sea prior to moving to wintering areas in the Bering Sea. MRPP did not distinguish any differences in distribution of wing molt locations by sex ($\delta_{59} = 0.41$, $P = 0.57$) or year ($\delta_{59} = 0.06$, $P = 0.44$).

Eiders wintered along the Chukotsk, Kamchatka, and Alaska Peninsulas, Olyutor and Bristol Bays, and the Gulf of Alaska (Table 2, Figure 6). MRPP did not distinguish any differences in distribution of winter locations by sex ($\delta_{29} = -0.82$, $P = 0.16$) or year ($\delta_{29} = 0.47$, $P = 0.59$).

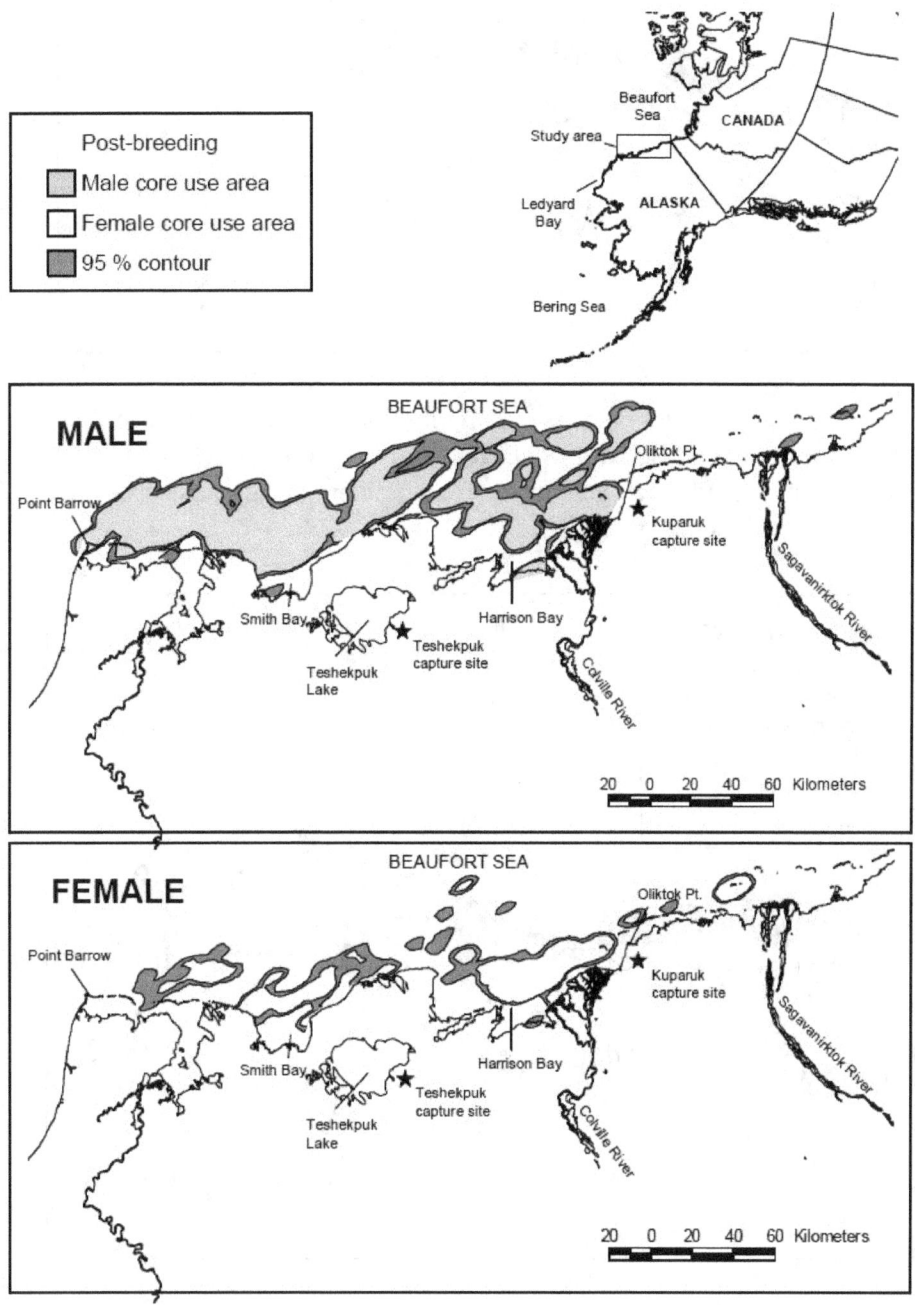

Figure 1. Post-breeding distributions of king eiders (34 male, 26 female) within the Alaskan Beaufort Sea, 2002–2004.

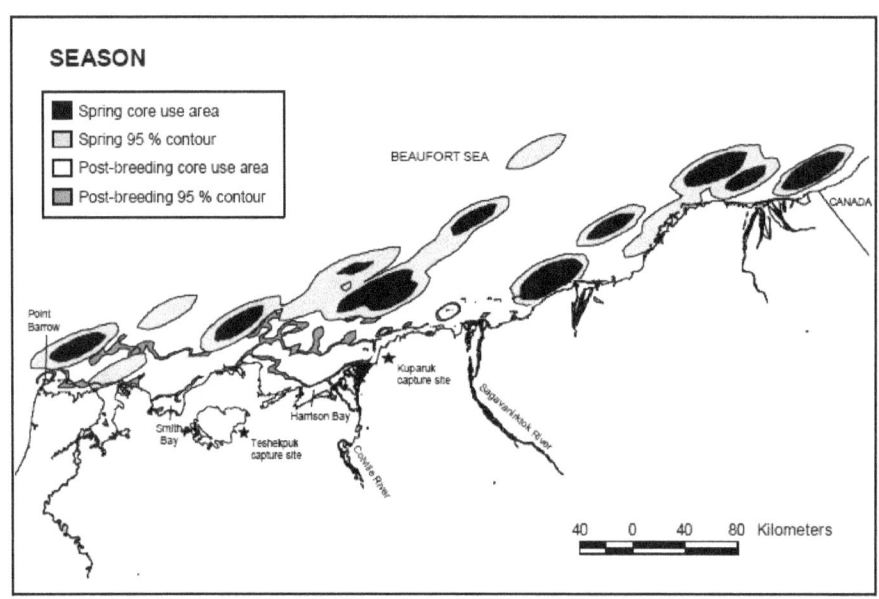

Figure 2. Post-breeding and spring distributions of satellite-tagged king eiders in the Alaskan Beaufort Sea, June 2002 – September 2004. Distributions include locations from 60 king eiders during post-breeding and 24 king eiders during spring.

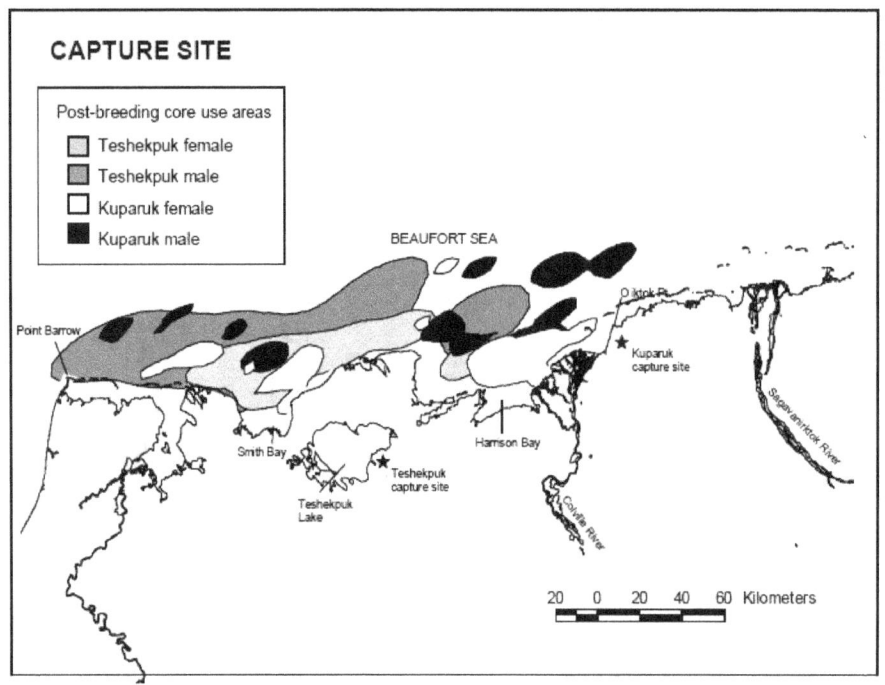

Figure 3. Post-breeding distributions within the Alaskan Beaufort Sea of king eiders captured at Kuparuk and Teshekpuk Lake on the North Slope of Alaska. Distributions include locations from 15 king eiders captured at Kuparuk and 12 king eiders captured at Teshekpuk Lake in 2004.

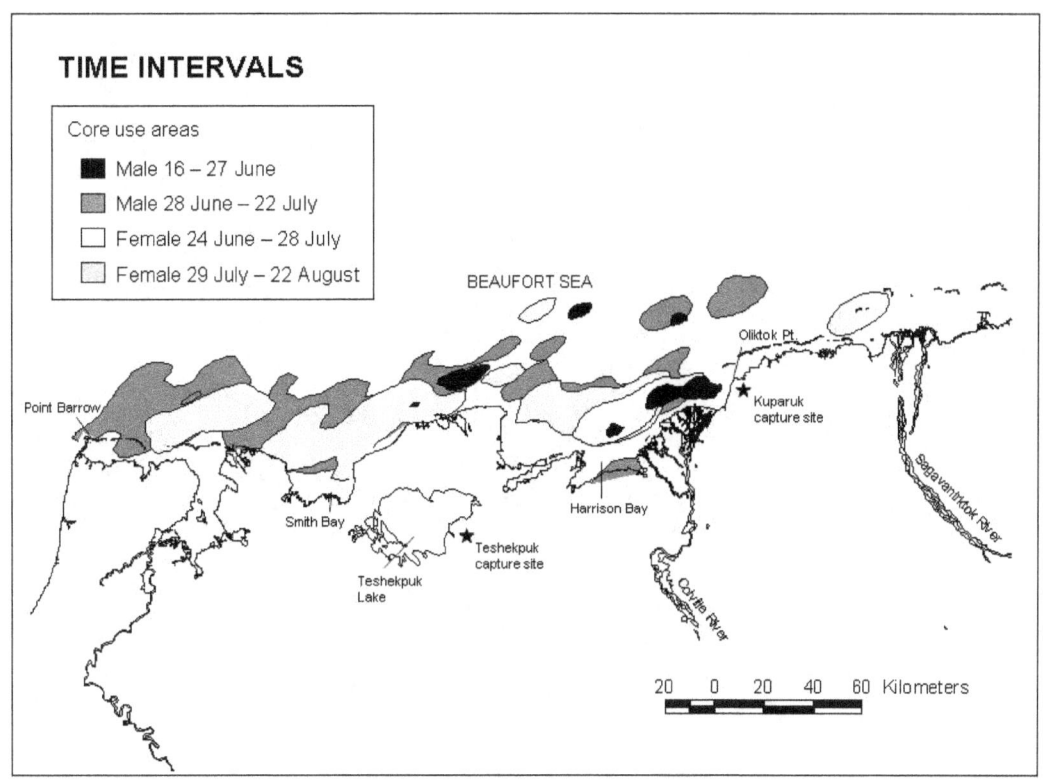

Figure 4. Staging areas of satellite transmittered king eiders during spring and wing molt migration.

Errata: Substitute the following figures for the ones on pages 16 and 17.

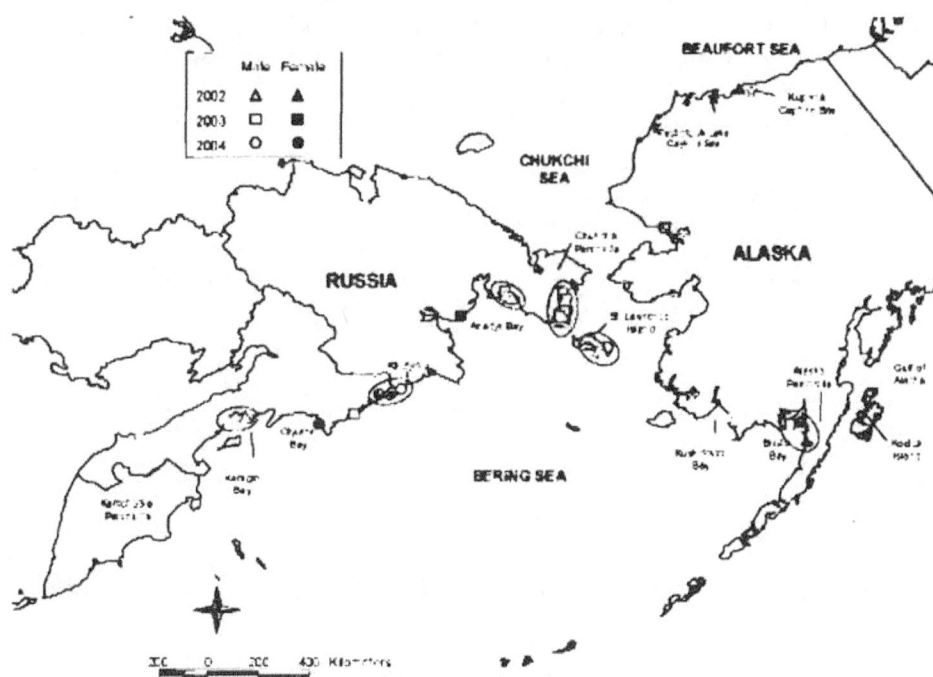

Figure 5. Distribution of 59 satellite transmittered king eiders during 2002 – 2004 wing molt periods. Areas occupied by two or more eider locations over the three years of the study are outlined by a dashed grey line.

Figure 6. Distribution of 29 satellite transmittered king eiders during 2002 – 2003 at farthest south wintering sites. Areas occupied by two or more eider locations over the two years of the study are outlined by a dashed grey line.

Table 2. Proportion of male and female satellite transmittered king eiders captured on the North Slope of Alaska located in major wing molt and wintering areas in 2002 – 2004.

Location	2002		2003		2004	
	Male	Female	Male	Female	Male	Female
WING MOLT AREA (n)	*(11)*	*(10)*	*(9)*	*(2)*	*(14)*	*(13)*
Russia						
Karagin Bay	*0.18*	*0.10*	*0*	*0*	*0*	*0*
Khatyrka	*0*	*0*	*0*	*0*	*0.14*	*0.15*
Anadyr Bay	*0.18*	*0.10*	*0.44*	*0*	*0.07*	*0.08*
Chukotsk Peninsula	*0.18*	*0.50*	*0.33*	*1.00*	*0.43*	*0.46*
Alaska						
St. Lawrence Island	*0.18*	*0.10*	*0*	*0*	*0.21*	*0.08*
Bristol Bay	*0*	*0.20*	*0.11*	*0*	*0.07*	*0.15*
WINTERING AREA (n)	*(10)*	*(8)*	*(9)*	*(2)*		
Russia						
Kamchatka Peninsula	*0.30*	*0*	*0.11*	*0*		
Olyutor Bay	*0.10*	*0.38*	*0.22*	*0*		
Chukotsk Peninsula	*0.10*	*0.12*	*0.22*	*0.50*		
Alaska						
Bristol Bay	*0.30*	*0*	*0*	*0*		
Alaska Peninsula	*0.10*	*0.38*	*0.33*	*0.50*		
Gulf of Alaska	*0.10*	*0.12*	*0*	*0*		

Movements

Mean dates of dispersal from breeding areas and arrival at wing molt sites differed by sex (dispersal from breeding: $F_{1,59} = 75.28$, $P < 0.001$; arrival at molt site: $F_{1,59} = 65.79$, $P < 0.001$) and among years (dispersal from breeding: $F_{2,59} = 7.18$, $P < 0.01$; arrival at molt site: $F_{2,59} = 3.98$, $P = 0.02$). Female eiders dispersed from breeding areas and arrived at wing molt sites later than males in all years (Table 3, Figure 7).

Average number of days at wing molt sites varied by year ($F_{2,55} = 4.99$, $P = 0.01$) with eiders spending significantly more days at wing molt sites in 2003 (74 ± 4 days) than either 2002 (57 ± 3 days) or 2004 (53 ± 2 days). Number of days at wing molt sites did not vary by sex ($F_{1,}$

$_{55}$ = 2.41, P = 0.13). Females dispersed from wing molt sites later than males ($F_{1, 55}$ = 5.57, P = 0.02, Table 3). Dispersal date from wing molt sites did not vary by year ($F_{2, 55}$ = 1.57, P = 0.22).

Arrival date at breeding areas the following year did not vary by sex ($F_{1, 18}$ = 1.64, P = 0.22) or year ($F_{2, 18}$ = 0.01, P = 0.92).

The year/sex interaction term was not significant in all previous two-way ANOVAs (P > 0.10).

Table 3. Mean and range of dispersal dates from breeding areas, arrival at wing molt sites, dispersal from wing molt sites, and arrival at subsequent breeding areas for 60 king eiders captured on the North Slope of Alaska in 2002 – 2004.

	Dispersal from breeding (n)	Range	Arrival at molt (n)	Range	Dispersal from molt (n)	Range	Arrival at breeding (n)	Range
SEX								
Male	23 Jun (33)	14 Jun – 4 Jul	31 Jul (33)	18 Jul – 2 Sep	2 Oct (33)	13 Sep – 12 Nov	12 Jun (12)	7 – 24 Jun
Female	14 Jul (27)	21 Jun – 8 Aug	28 Aug (27)	5 Aug – 13 Sep	17 Oct (23)	16 Sep – 9 Nov	11 Jun (7)	7 – 12 Jun
YEAR								
2002	29 Jun (21)	14 Jun – 26 Jul	10 Aug (21)	21 Jul – 8 Sep	5 Oct (19)	16 Sep – 9 Nov	11 Jun (12)	7 – 24 Jun
2003	30 Jun (12)	20 Jun – 30 Jul	8 Aug (12)	18 Jul – 4 Sep	15 Oct (11)	23 Sep – 12 Nov	12 Jun (7)	6 – 23 Jun
2004	6 Jul (27)	19 Jun – 7 Aug	16 Aug (27)	27 Jul – 12 Sep	8 Oct (26)	12 Sep – 29 Oct	NA	NA
ALL	3 Jul (60)	14 Jun – 8 Aug	13 Aug (60)	18 Jul – 13 Sep	9 Oct (56)	13 Sep – 12 Nov	12 Jun (19)	7 – 24 Jun

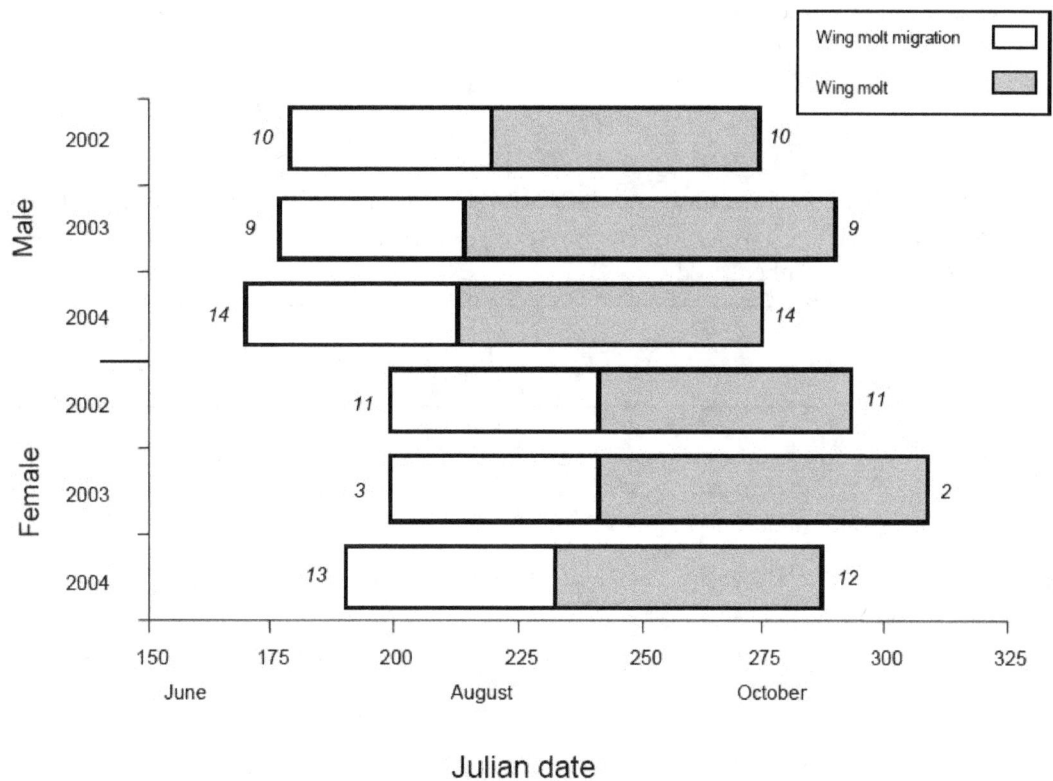

Figure 7. Mean number of days spent on wing molt migration and at wing molt sites for satellite transmittered king eiders for years 2002 – 2004. Sample sizes for the number of individual eiders used to calculate mean days of wing molt migration and duration at wing molt sites are represented respectively by the italicized number on the left and right sides of the bars, respectively. Ranges associated with dates of dispersal from breeding areas, arrival at wing molt sites, and dispersal from wing molt sites are found in Table 3.

Beaufort Sea Location Characteristics

Water depth at king eider locations differed by sex ($F_{1,548} = 16.68$, $P < 0.001$) and season ($F_{1,548} = 20.12$, $P < 0.001$) with a significant interaction between sex and season ($F_{1,548} = 42.65$, $P < 0.001$. During the post-breeding period, females were in shallower water (11.7 ± 0.8 m) than males (12.6 ± 0.4).) During spring migration, female locations were in deeper water (28.8 ± 3.1 m) than male locations (11.1 ± 1.8).

Significant variation in residence time of transmittered king eiders within the Beaufort Sea was explained by sex ($t_{1,69} = -2.98$, $P = 0.004$), season ($t_{1,69} = 3.66$, $P < 0.001$), and standardized Julian date of first location within the sea ($t_{1,69} = -4.89$, $P < 0.001$, Figure 8). Year ($t_{1,69} = -0.35$, $P = 0.728$), sex*year ($t_{1,69} = -0.06$, $P = 0.956$), sex*season ($t_{1,69} = -0.88$, $P = 0.383$), and sex*Julian date ($t_{1,69} = 1.90$, $P = 0.062$) explained little variation in residence times. Females moved into the Beaufort Sea almost 2 weeks later than males in the spring and 20 days later than males during the post-breeding periods (Table 4, Figure 9). They spent almost twice as many

21

days on average in the sea than males in spring and more than a week longer than males during post-breeding (Table 4, Figure 9).

Table 4. Mean (± SE) residence time and date of first location within the Alaskan Beaufort Sea of transmittered king eiders during post-breeding (n = 60 eiders) and spring migration (n = 24 eiders), June 2002 – September 2004.

Residence time (days)	MALE		FEMALE	
	Mean	*Range*	*Mean*	*Range*
Post-breeding	*18.2 ± 1.6*	*1 – 48*	*26.9 ± 2.4*	*14 – 62*
Spring	*7.3 ± 2.9*	*1 – 15*	*13 ± 3.7*	*4 – 20*
Date				
Post-breeding	*25 Jun*	*16 Jun – 4 Jul*	*15 Jul*	*18 Jun – 8 Aug*
Spring	*13 May*	*30 Apr – 20 May*	*26 May*	*17 May – 8 Jun*

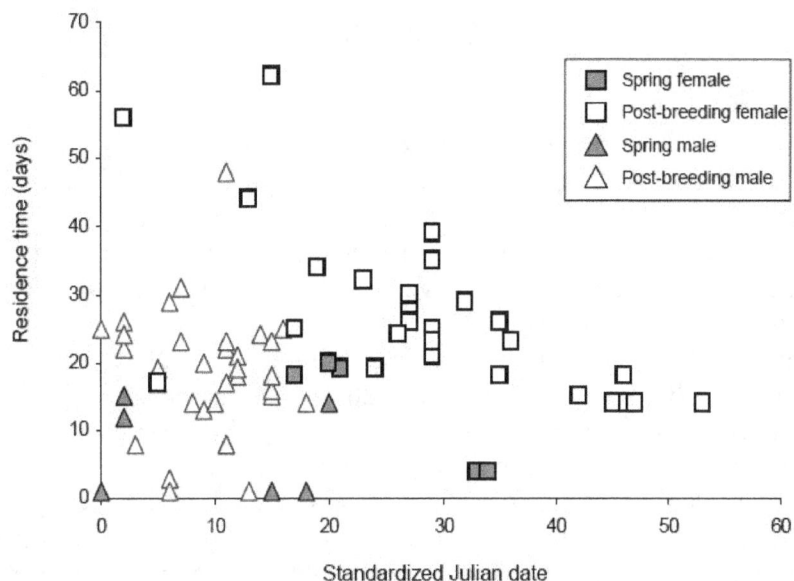

Figure 8. Plot of residence time and standardized date of arrival in the Alaskan Beaufort Sea of king eiders ($n = 60$) during spring and post-breeding periods.

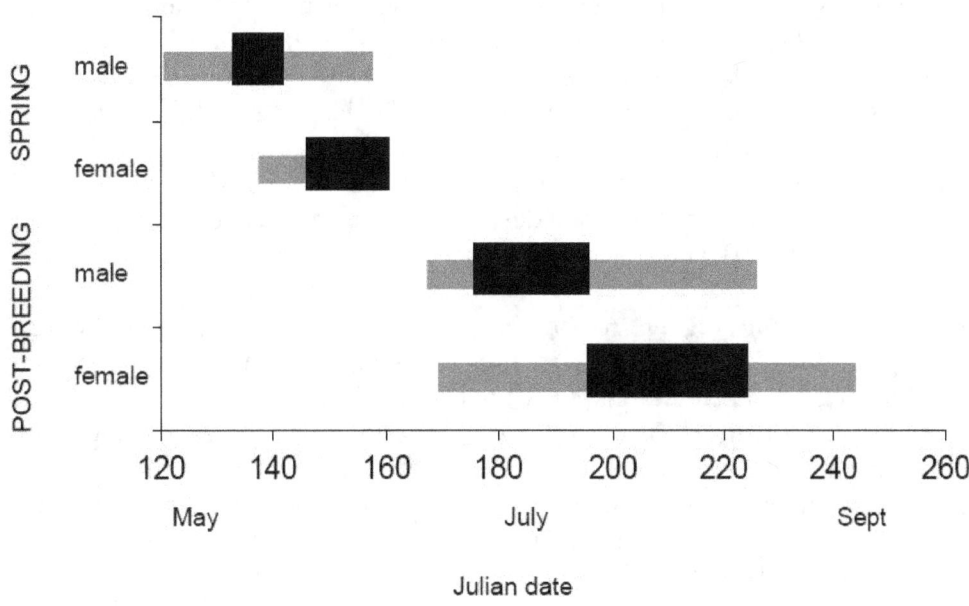

Figure 9. Mean range of residence time (days, dark bar) and range (grey bar) transmittered king eiders in the Alaskan Beaufort Sea during spring and post-breeding periods.

DISCUSSION

Distribution and Use Areas

Beaufort Sea. Hundreds of thousands of king eiders pass through the Beaufort Sea each year during post-breeding and spring migrations (Suydam et al. 2000). Every king eider we transmittered on the North Slope of Alaska spent at least 1 day in the Alaskan Beaufort Sea after the breeding season. More than 80% of our transmittered eiders spent more than 2 weeks staging offshore prior to beginning molt migration, suggesting that the sea is an important migration flyway and staging area for this species.

Concentrations of eiders at Harrison Bay and Smith Bay in July were consistent with the findings of Fischer et al. (2002) and Dickson et al. (2000). During post-breeding aerial surveys of the central Beaufort Sea, Fischer et al. (2002) recorded their highest densities of king eiders in deep water (>10 m) areas of Harrison Bay in July. Stehn and Platte (2000) analyzed these same aerial survey data and calculated a density of 3.6 king eiders per km^2 in the deep water (>8 m) area from the Kogru River to Oliktok Point. Dickson et al. (2000) described Harrison and Smith Bays as summer staging areas for king eiders transmittered on breeding grounds at Victoria Island, Northwest Territories and Prudhoe Bay, Alaska.

In this study, Smith Bay was an area used more heavily by post-breeding female eiders than male eiders. Troy (2003) found the area around Smith Bay to be an important use area for North Slope-breeding female spectacled eiders (*Somateria fischeri*). After leaving the breeding grounds, 90% of his tagged females spent over 70% of their time in and around Smith Bay prior to departing the Beaufort Sea. He speculated that high ice cover in Smith Bay early in the post-breeding period prevented male spectacled eiders from using this area. Severe ice conditions early in the summer may also have reduced the amount of time transmittered male king eiders spent in Smith Bay. Shore-fast ice in the Beaufort Sea generally begins to move offshore in early July creating open water habitat nearshore (Craig et al. 1984). The broad distribution of male locations in the sea after breeding may reflect high (>75%) ice cover in June which forces male king eiders to dispersed pockets of open water during post-breeding.

Post-breeding and spring distribution of king eider locations in the Alaskan Beaufort Sea overlapped very little. Short residence times and deep water at spring locations suggest that king eiders may be using the Alaskan Beaufort Sea as a migration corridor rather than a staging area during this period.

Post-breeding and spring staging. As mentioned above, king eiders staged more than two weeks on average in the Beaufort Sea after breeding. Staging areas outside the Beaufort Sea included Ledyard Bay in the Chukchi Sea and the Chukotsk Peninsula. Dickson et al. (2000) described the northern part of Ledyard Bay near Icy Cape as a fall staging area for king eiders transmittered in Canada migrating to wing molt sites in the Bering Sea.

During spring migration, our transmittered king eiders that returned to breed in Alaska and western Canada did not appear to stage within the Alaskan Beaufort Sea. Ledyard Bay may be a more critical stopover area during spring migration for foraging and resting.

Wing molt and winter. Unlike spectacled and Steller's eiders (*Polysticta stelleri*) (Petersen 1980, Petersen et al. 1999), male and female king eiders exhibited no sexual segregation of wing molt sites. The apparent lack of successfully breeding females in this study may explain our inability to detect any sexual segregation. During the course of the study, we found three of our transmittered hens incubating eggs, but timing of dispersal from breeding areas suggested none successfully fledged young. There is some evidence that female eiders that successfully raise young to fledging may molt flight feathers closer to the breeding grounds (Petersen et al. 1999), possibly in terrestrial environments (Knoche 2004). The distribution of wintering sites also did not differ between male and female king eiders. This lack of sexual segregation would be predicted for waterfowl species that, like king eider, form pair bonds on wintering grounds (Hepp and Hair 1984) or use marine habitat during winter (Diefenbach et al. 1988).

Wing molt sites for king eiders in this study were similar to those found by Dickson et al. (2000), with the addition of molting areas located in the Alaskan Beaufort Sea, Olyutor Bay, and on the west side of the Kamchatka Peninsula. We found additional wintering areas in Olyutor Bay, at the southern most tip of the Kamchatka Peninsula, and in Anadyr Bay. Both wing molt and wintering sites for our sample of king eiders were widely dispersed along the coastline of the Bering Sea supporting the results of Pearce et al. (2003) which revealed little spatial genetic structure within this population.

Movements

For Alaskan-breeding king eiders, differences between sexes in dispersal dates from breeding grounds, arrival dates at wing molt sites, and departure dates from wing molt sites were consistent with those captured in western Canada (Dickson et al. 2000), king eiders molting flight feathers in Greenland (Frimer 1994), and with other eider species (Petersen 1981, Petersen et al. 1999). The later chronology of molt migration in 2004 suggests inter-year variation in the timing of wing molt in king eiders. The interrelationship of reproductive and wing molt periods in waterfowl has been demonstrated previously, and annual variation in the timing of nesting tends to affect the molt chronology of females more than males (Leafloor and Ankney 1989, Hohman et al. 1992). Postbreeding female waterfowl may have less time for premigratory fattening, potentially leading to a cascading delay in timing of arrival at wing molt, wintering, and breeding sites the following year (Hohman et al. 1992).

Beaufort Sea Location Characteristics

The earlier timing of male king eiders in the Beaufort Sea relative to females is consistent with previous eider studies (Petersen et al. 1999, Dickson et al. 2000, Troy 2003). Male king eiders disperse from breeding grounds at the onset of incubation, while female timing is probably dependent on her success or failure as a breeder. Males spent fewer days staging in the Beaufort Sea post-breeding than females. Female king eiders may need to remain in the Beaufort Sea longer than males prior to molt migration to replenish fat stores depleted during egg-laying and incubation. Female eiders rely on endogenous reserves for egg-laying and forage very little while incubating (Korschgen 1977, Kellet 1999). King eiders nesting at Karrak Lake, Northwest Territories lost 32% of their pre-incubation body mass during incubation (Kellet 1999).

We found no apparent trend of residence time with date of arrival for male king eiders and the opposite trend for females. Timing of female staging and migration in the Beaufort Sea may be constrained by subsequent life history events. Female ducks with longer reproductive efforts may have limited time to replenish diminished fat stores before beginning molt migration, especially in the high arctic where advancing winter weather could reduce forage quality or entrap flightless birds in advancing ice at wing molt sites (Salomonsen 1968, Hohman et al.

1992). In spring, early arrival on breeding grounds may provide reproductive advantages to nesting female waterfowl (Johnson et al. 1992). Timing of male molt migration appears to be highly synchronized in most waterfowl (Hohman et al. 1992), and this is supported by the behavior of our transmittered male eiders after breeding.

ACKNOWLEDGEMENTS

Financial support for this research was provided by Coastal Marine Institute (University of Alaska, Fairbanks) and Minerals Management Service. Additional support was provided by ConocoPhillips, Alaska, Inc., the North Slope Borough, U.S.G.S. Alaska Cooperative Fish and Wildlife Research Unit, Sea Duck Joint Venture, UA Foundation- Angus Gavin grant, Institute of Arctic Biology, and U.S. Fish and Wildlife Service. We would like to acknowledge the valuable input and technical assistance provided by C. Monnett, J. Gleason, B. Anderson, P. Martin, T. Obritschkewitsch, C. Rea, A. Lazenby, L. McDaniel, J. Harth, D. Douglas, R. Suydam, D. Troy, P. Howey, B. Griffith, F. Huettmann, and C. MacIntyre. For assistance trapping eiders, we would like to thank E. Duran, L. Guildehaus, A. Prevel, K. Roby, R. Acker, S. Backensto, C. Adler, R. McGuire, and M. Knoche. L. Dickson, J. Gleason and an anonymous reviewer provided helpful comments on this paper. We are also grateful to our veterinarian C. Scott and veterinary technicians K. Adams and M. Carlson for performing the surgeries. Use of brand names within this report does not imply endorsement by U.S.G.S.

STUDY PRODUCTS

Presentations:

Phillips, L., A. Powell, E. Taylor. 2005. Use of the Beaufort Sea by king eiders. 10th Annual MMS Information Transfer Meeting, Anchorage, AK.

Powell, A. N., E. Rexstad, E. Taylor, and L. Phillips. 2005. Importance of the Beaufort Sea to king eiders (*Somateria spectabilis*). CMI Annual Review, University of Alaska, Fairbanks, AK (L Phillips, presenter).

Phillips, L. and A. N. Powell. 2005. Large-scale movements and habitat use of king eiders throughout the nonbreeding season. Annual Meeting, Pacific Seabird Group/Waterbird Society Meeting, 19–23 January, Portland, OR.

Phillips, L., A. N. Powell, and E. Taylor. 2004. Molt migration and ecology of king eiders. Annual Meeting, American Ornithologists Union, 16–21 August, Quebec City, QC, Canada.

Phillips. L. A., A. N. Powell, and E. Taylor. 2004. Migration ecology of king eiders. Alaska Forum on the Environment, Anchorage, AK.

Phillips, L., A. N. Powell, and E. Taylor. 2004. Migration ecology of king eiders. CMI Annual Review, University of Alaska, Fairbanks, AK.

Phillips, L., R. McGuire, and M. Knoche. 2004. Alaska's eiders. Presentation at Alaska Bird Observatory' seminar series.

Phillips, L., A. N. Powell, and E. Taylor. 2003. Importance of the Beaufort Sea to King Eiders. CMI Annual Review, University of Alaska, Fairbanks, AK.

Phillips, L. M., A. N. Powell, and E. J Taylor. 2002. Importance of the Alaskan Beaufort Sea to king eiders during fall migration. Poster; North American Sea Duck Conference, 6–10 November 2002, Victoria, B.C.

Powell, A. N. 2002. Ecology of King Eiders on Alaska's North Slope. MMS Information Transfer Seminar, Anchorage, AK.

Reports:

Phillips, L. M. 2005. Migration ecology and distribution of king eiders. M.S. Thesis, University of Alaska, Fairbanks, AK.

Powell, A. N., L. M. Phillips. E. A. Rexstad, and E. J. Taylor. 2004. Importance of the Alaskan Beaufort Sea to king eiders (*Somateria spectabilis*). Annual Report, CMI, University of Alaska, Fairbanks, AK.

Powell, A. N., E. Taylor, E. Rexstad, and L. Phillips. 2004. Importance of the Alaskan Beaufort Sea to King Eiders. Report to the Sea Duck Joint Venture. http://www.seaduckjv.org/ssna.html

Powell, A. N., L. M. Phillips. E. A. Rexstad, and E. J. Taylor. 2003. Importance of the Alaskan Beaufort Sea to king eiders (*Somateria spectabilis*). Annual Report, CMI, University of Alaska, Fairbanks, AK.

Powell, A. N., E. Taylor, E. Rexstad, and L. Phillips. 2003. Importance of the Alaskan Beaufort Sea to king eiders. Report to the Sea Duck Joint Venture. http://www.seaduckjv.org/ssna.html

Powell, A. N., L. M. Phillips. E. A. Rexstad, and E. J. Taylor. 2002. Importance of the Alaskan Beaufort Sea to king eiders (*Somateria spectabilis*). Annual Report, CMI, University of Alaska, Fairbanks, AK.

LITERATURE CITED

Alaska Science Center. 1997. Coastal Bathymetry of the Bering, Chukchi, and Beaufort. <http://www.absc.usgs.gov/research/walrus/bering/bathy/nosbath-meta.htm> (January 2005).

Anderson, M. G., J. M. Rhymer, and F. C. Rohwer. 1992. Philopatry, dispersal and the genetic structure of waterfowl populations. p. 365–395. *In* B. D. J. Batt, A. D. Afton, M. G. Anderson, C. D. Ankney, D. H. Johnson, J. A. Kadlec, and G. L. Krapu [eds.], Ecology and management of breeding waterfowl. University of Minnesota Press, Minneapolis, MN.

Barnes, P. W., D. M. Rearic, and E. Riemnitz. 1984. Ice gouging characteristics and processes. Pages 185–212 *in* P. W. Barnes, D. M. Schell, and E. Reimnitz, editors. The Alaskan Beaufort Sea: Ecosystem and environment. Academic Press, Inc., Orlando, Florida, USA.

Cade, B. S., and J. D. Richards. 2001. User manual for BLOSSOM statistical software. U. S. Geological Survey Midcontinent Ecological Science Center, Fort Collins, CO.

Craig, P. C., W. B. Griffiths, S. R. Johnson., and D. M. Schell. 1984. Trophic dynamics in an arctic lagoon. Pages 347–380 *in* P. W. Barnes, D. M. Schell, and E. Reimnitz, editors. The Alaskan Beaufort Sea: Ecosystem and environment. Academic Press, Inc., Orlando, Florida, USA.

Dickson, D. L., R. S. Suydam, and G. Balogh. 2000. Tracking the movements of king eiders from nesting grounds at Prudhoe Bay, Alaska to their molting and wintering areas using satellite telemetry. Canadian Wildlife Service, Environment Canada, Edmonton, Alberta, Canada.

Diefenbach, D. R., J. D. Nichols, and J. E. Hines. 1988. Distribution patterns during winter and fidelity to wintering areas of American Black Zoology 66:1506–1513.

Dugger, B. D. 1997. Factors influencing the onset of spring migration in Mallards. Journal of Field Ornithology 68:331–337.

ESRI. 1998. ArcView GIS Version 3.3. Environmental Research Institute, Inc., Redlands, California, USA.

Fay, F. H. 1974. The role of ice in the ecology of marine mammals of the Bering Sea. p. 383–399. *In* D. W. Hood, and E. J. Kelley [eds.], Oceanography of the Bering Sea with emphasis on renewable resources. Proceedings of the International Symposium for Bering Sea Study.

Fischer, J. B., T. J. Tiplady, and W. W. Larned. 2002. Monitoring Beaufort Sea waterfowl and marine birds, aerial survey component. U. S. Fish and Wildlife Service, Division of Migratory Bird Management, Anchorage, Alaska, USA.

Flint, P. L., A. C. Fowler, and R. F. Rockwell. 1999. Modeling bird mortality associated with the M/V Citrus oil spill off St. Paul Island, Alaska. Ecological Modelling 117:261–267.

Frimer, O. 1994. Autumn arrival and moult in King Eiders (*Somateria spectabilis*) at Disco, West Greenland. Arctic 47:137–141.

Frimer, O. 1997. Diet of moulting King Eiders *Somateria spectabilis* at Disco Island, West Greenland. Ornis Fennica 74:187–194.

Gauthreaux, S. A. 1985. The temporal and spatial scales of migration in relation to environmental changes in time and space. p. 503–515. *In* M. A. Rankin [eds.], Migration: mechanisms and adaptive significance. Marine Science Institute. The University of Texas at Austin, Port Aransas, TX.

Grebmeier, J. M. 1993. Studies of pelagic-benthic coupling extended onto the Soviet continental shelf in the northern Bering and Chukchi seas. Continental Shelf Research. 13:653–668.

Heitmeyer, M. E., and L. H. Fredrickson. 1981. Do wetland conditions in the Mississippi Delta hardwoods influence Mallard recruitment? Transactions of the North American Wildlife and Natural Resources Conference 46:44–57.

Heitemeyer, M. E. 1988. Body composition of female Mallards in winter in relation to annual cycle events. Condor 90:669–680.

Hepp, G. R. 1984. Dominance in wintering Anatinae: potential effects on clutch size and time of nesting. Wildfowl 35:132–134.

Hepp, G. R., and J. D. Hair. 1984. Dominance of wintering waterfowl (Anatini): effects on distribution of sexes. Condor 86:251–257.

Hohman, W. L., C. D. Ankney, and D. H. Gordon. 1992. Ecology and management of postbreeding waterfowl. Pages 128–189 *in* B. D. J. Batt, A. D. Afton, M. G. Anderson, C. D. Ankney, D. H. Johnson, J. A. Kadlec, and G. L. Krapu, editors. Ecology and management of breeding waterfowl. University of Minnesota Press, Minneapolis, Minnesota, USA.

Hooge, P. N., and B. Eichenlaub [online]. 1997. Animal movement extension to ArcView. Ver 1.1. <http://www.absc.usgs.gov/glba/gistools/> (January 2005).

Johnson, D. H., J. D. Nichols, and M. D. Schwartz. 1992. Population dynamics of breeding waterfowl. Pages 446–475. *in* B. D. J. Batt, A. D. Afton, M. G. Anderson, C. D. Ankney, D. H. Johnson, J. A. Kadlec, and G. L. Krapu, editors. Ecology and management of breeding waterfowl. University of Minnesota Press, Minneapolis, Minnesota, USA.

Kellet, D. K. 1999. Causes and consequences of variation in nest success of king eiders (*Somateria spectabilis*) at Karrak Lake, Northwest Territories. M. S. thesis, University of Saskatchewan, Saskatoon, Canada.

Kertell, K. 1991. Disappearance of the Steller's Eider from the Yukon-Kuskokwim Delta, Alaska. Arctic 44:177–187.

King, J. R. 1974. Seasonal allocation of time and energy resources in birds. p. 4–83. *In* R. A. Paynter, Jr. [eds.], Avian energetics. Nuttal Ornithological Club. Cambridge, MA.

Knoche M. J. 2004. King eider wing molt and migration: Inferences from stable carbon and nitrogen isotopes. M.S. thesis. University of Alaska, Fairbanks.

Korschgen, C. E. 1977. Breeding stress of female eiders in Maine. Journal of Wildlife Management 41:360–373.

Korschgen, C. E., K. P. Kenow, A. Gendron-Fitzpatrick, W. L. Green, and F. J. Dein. 1996. Implanting intra-abdominal radiotransmitters with external whip antennas in ducks. Journal of Wildlife Management 60:132–137.

Leafloor, J. O., and C. D. Ankney. 1989. Factors affecting wing molt chronology of female mallards. Canadian Journal of Zoology 69:924–928.

Niebauer, A. J., N. A. Bond, L. P. Yakunin, and V. V. Plotnikov. 1999. An update on the climatology and sea ice of the Bering Sea. p. 29–60. *In* T. R. Loughlin and K. Ohtani [eds.], Dynamics of the Bering Sea. University of Alaska Sea Grant, Fairbanks, AK.

Norton, D., and G. Weller.1984. The Beaufort Sea: Background, history and perspective. Pages 3–19 *in* P. W. Barnes, D. M. Schell, and E. Reimnitz, editors. The Alaskan Beaufort Sea: Ecosystem and environment. Academic Press, Inc., Orlando, Florida, USA.

Pearce, J. M., S. L. Talbot, B. J. Pierson, M. R. Petersen, K. T. Scribner, D. L. Dickson, and A. Mosbech. 2003. Lack of spatial genetic structure among nesting and wintering King Eiders. Condor 106:229–240.

Petersen, M. R. 1980. Observations of wing-feather moult and summer feeding ecology of Steller's Eiders at Nelson Lagoon, Alaska. Wildfowl 31:99–106.

Petersen, M. R. 1981. Populations, feeding ecology and molt of Steller's Eiders. Condor 83:256–262.

Petersen, M. R., W. W. Larned, and D. C. Douglas. 1999. At-sea distribution of spectacled eiders: A 120-year-old mystery resolved. Auk 116:1009–1020.

Petersen, M. R., and D. C. Douglas. 2004. Winter ecology of Spectacled Eiders: environmental characteristics and population change. Condor 106:79–94.

Salomonsen, F. 1968. The moult migration. Wildfowl 19:5–24.

SAS Institute. 1990: SAS user's guide: statistics. Version 8. SAS Institute, Inc. Cary, North Carolina, USA.

Seaman, D. E., B. Griffith, and R. A. Powell. 1998. KERNELHR: a program for estimating animal home ranges. Wildlife Society Bulletin 26:95–100.

Sea Duck Joint Venture Management Board. 2001. Sea Duck Joint Venture Strategic Plan: 2001–2006. SDJV Continental Technical Team. Unpublished Report.

Service Argos. 2001. Argos user's manual. Service Argos, Inc., Largo, Maryland, USA. <http://www.cls.fr/manuel/> (January 2005).

Soluri, E. A., and V. A. Woodson. 1990. World vector shoreline. <http://rimmer.ngdc.noaa.gov/mgg/coast/wvs/> (January 2005).

Springer, A. M., and C. P. McRoy. 1993. The paradox of pelagic food webs in the northern Bering Sea-III. Patterns of primary production. Continental Shelf Research 13:575–599.

Stehn, R. A., C. P. Dau, B. Conant, and W. I. Butler. 1993. Decline of spectacled eiders nesting in western Alaska. Arctic 46:264–277.

Stehn, R., and R. Platte. 2000. Exposure of birds to assumed oil spills at the Liberty Project. U.S. Fish and Wildlife Service, Division of Migratory Bird Management, Anchorage, Alaska, USA.

Stringer, W. J., and J. E. Groves. 1991. Location and areal extent of polynyas in the Bering and Chukchi Seas. Arctic 44:164–171.

Suydam, R. S. 2000. King eider (*Somateria spectabilis*). *in* A. Poole, and F. Gill, editors. The Birds of North America. The Birds of North America, Inc., Philadelphia, Pennsylvania, USA.

Suydam, R. S., D. L. Dickson, J. B. Fadely, and L. T. Quakenbush. 2000. Population declines of king and common eiders of the Beaufort Sea. Condor 102:219–222.

Systad, G. H., J. O. Bustnes, and K. E. Erikstad. 2000. Behavioral responses to decreasing day length in wintering sea ducks. Auk 117:33–40.

Thomson, D. Q., and R. A. Person. 1963. The eider pass at Point Barrow, Alaska. Journal of Wildlife Management 27:348–355.

Troy, D. 2003. Molt migration of spectacled eiders in the Beaufort Sea region. Troy Ecological Research Associates, Anchorage, Alaska, USA.

U. S. Fish and Wildlife Service. 1999. Population status and trends of sea ducks in Alaska. Migratory Bird Management, Waterfowl Management Branch. Unpublished Report.

Walsh, J. J., C. P. McRoy, L. K. Coachman, J. J. Goering, J. J. Nihoul, T. E. Whitledge, T. H. Blackburn, P. L. Parker, C. D. Wirik, P. G. Shuert, J. M. Grebmeier, A. M. Springer, R.

D. Tripp, D. A. Hansell, S. Djenidi, E. Deleersnijdeer, K. Henriksen, B. A. Lund, P. Andersen, F. E. Muller-Karger, and K. Dean. 1989. Carbon and nitrogen cycling within the Bering/Chukchi seas: source regions for organic matter effecting AOU demands of the Arctic Ocean. Progress in Oceanography 22:277–359.

Woodby, D. A., and G. J. Divoky. 1982. Spring migration of eiders and other waterbirds at Point Barrow, Alaska. Arctic 35:403–410.